LAYERS OF LEARNING

YEAR ONE • UNIT SEVEN

PHOENICIANS

OCEANS

MOTION

MORAL STORIES

HooDoo Publishing
United States of America
©2014 Layers of Learning
Copies of maps or activities may be made for a particular family or classroom.
ISBN 978-1494722906

Units At A Glance: Topics For All Four Years of the Layers of Learning Program

1	History	Geography	Science	The Arts
1	Mesopotamia	Maps & Globes	Planets	Cave Paintings
2	Egypt	Map Keys	Stars	Egyptian Art
3	Europe	Global Grids	Earth & Moon	Crafts
4	Ancient Greece	Wonders	Satellites	Greek Art
5	Babylon	Mapping People	Humans in Space	Poetry
6	The Levant	Physical Earth	Laws of Motion	List Poems
7	Phoenicians	Oceans	Motion	Moral Stories
8	Assyrians	Deserts	Fluids	Rhythm
9	Persians	Arctic	Waves	Melody
10	Ancient China	Forests	Machines	Chinese Art
11	Early Japan	Mountains	States of Matter	Line & Shape
12	Arabia	Rivers & Lakes	Atoms	Color & Value
13	Ancient India	Grasslands	Elements	Texture & Form
14	Ancient Africa	Africa	Bonding	African Tales
15	First North Americans	North America	Salts	Creative Kids
16	Ancient South America	South America	Plants	South American Art
17	Celts	Europe	Flowering Plants	Jewelry
18	Roman Republic	Asia	Trees	Roman Art
19	Christianity	Australia & Oceania	Simple Plants	Instruments
20	Roman Empire	You Explore	Fungi	Composing Music

2	History	Geography	Science	The Arts
1	Byzantines	Turkey	Climate & Seasons	Byzantine Art
2	Barbarians	Ireland	Forecasting	Illumination
3	Islam	Arabian Peninsula	Clouds & Precipitation	Creative Kids
4	Vikings	Norway	Special Effects	Viking Art
5	Anglo Saxons	Britain	Wild Weather	King Arthur Tales
6	Charlemagne	France	Cells and DNA	Carolingian Art
7	Normans	Nigeria	Skeletons	Canterbury Tales
8	Feudal System	Germany	Muscles, Skin, & Cardiopulmonary	Gothic Art
9	Crusades	Balkans	Digestive & Senses	Religious Art
10	Burgundy, Venice, Spain	Switzerland	Nerves	Oil Paints
11	Wars of the Roses	Russia	Health	Minstrels & Plays
12	Eastern Europe	Hungary	Metals	Printmaking
13	African Kingdoms	Mali	Carbon Chem	Textiles
14	Asian Kingdoms	Southeast Asia	Non-metals	Vivid Language
15	Mongols	Caucasus	Gases	Fun With Poetry
16	Medieval China & Japan	China	Electricity	Asian Arts
17	Pacific Peoples	Micronesia	Circuits	Arts of the Islands
18	American Peoples	Canada	Technology	Indian Legends
19	The Renaissance	Italy	Magnetism	Renaissance Art I
20	Explorers	Caribbean Sea	Motors	Renaissance Art II

3	History	Geography	Science	The Arts
1	Age of Exploration	Argentina and Chile	Classification & Insects	Fairy Tales
2	The Ottoman Empire	Egypt and Libya	Reptiles & Amphibians	Poetry
3	Mogul Empire	Pakistan & Afghanistan	Fish	Mogul Arts
4	Reformation	Angola & Zambia	Birds	Reformation Art
5	Renaissance England	Tanzania & Kenya	Mammals & Primates	Shakespeare
6	Thirty Years' War	Spain	Sound	Baroque Music
7	The Dutch	Netherlands	Light & Optics	Baroque Art I
8	France	Indonesia	Bending Light	Baroque Art II
9	The Enlightenment	Korean Pen.	Color	Art Journaling
10	Russia & Prussia	Central Asia	History of Science	Watercolors
11	Conquistadors	Baltic States	Igneous Rocks	Creative Kids
12	Settlers	Peru & Bolivia	Sedimentary Rocks	Native American Art
13	13 Colonies	Central America	Metamorphic Rocks	Settler Sayings
14	Slave Trade	Brazil	Gems & Minerals	Colonial Art
15	The South Pacific	Australasia	Fossils	Principles of Art
16	The British in India	India	Chemical Reactions	Classical Music
17	Boston Tea Party	Japan	Reversible Reactions	Folk Music
18	Founding Fathers	Iran	Compounds & Solutions	Rococo
19	Declaring Independence	Samoa and Tonga	Oxidation & Reduction	Creative Crafts I
20	The American Revolution	South Africa	Acids & Bases	Creative Crafts II

4	History	Geography	Science	The Arts
1	American Government	USA	Heat & Temperature	Patriotic Music
2	Expanding Nation	Pacific States	Motors & Engines	Tall Tales
3	Industrial Revolution	U.S. Landscapes	Energy	Romantic Art I
4	Revolutions	Mountain West States	Energy Sources	Romantic Art II
5	Africa	U.S. Political Maps	Energy Conversion	Impressionism I
6	The West	Southwest States	Earth Structure	Impressionism II
7	Civil War	National Parks	Plate Tectonics	Post-Impressionism
8	World War I	Plains States	Earthquakes	Expressionism
9	Totalitarianism	U.S. Economics	Volcanoes	Abstract Art
10	Great Depression	Heartland States	Mountain Building	Kinds of Art
11	World War II	Symbols and Landmarks	Chemistry of Air & Water	War Art
12	Modern East Asia	The South States	Food Chemistry	Modern Art
13	India's Independence	People of America	Industry	Pop Art
14	Israel	Appalachian States	Chemistry of Farming	Modern Music
15	Cold War	U.S. Territories	Chemistry of Medicine	Free Verse
16	Vietnam War	Atlantic States	Food Chains	Photography
17	Latin America	New England States	Animal Groups	Latin American Art
18	Civil Rights	Home State Study	Instincts	Theater & Film
19	Technology	Home State Study II	Habitats	Architecture
20	Terrorism	America in Review	Conservation	Creative Kids

Unit 1-7 printable pack

This unit includes printables at the end. To make life easier for you we also created digital printable packs for each unit. To retrieve your printable pack for Unit 1-7, please visit

www.layers-of-learning.com/digital-printable-packs/

Put the printable pack in your shopping cart and use this coupon code:

1216UNIT1-7

Your printable pack will be free.

LAYERS OF LEARNING INTRODUCTION

This is part of a series of units in the Layers of Learning homeschool curriculum, including the subjects of history, geography, science, and the arts. Children from 1st through 12th can participate in the same curriculum at the same time - family school style.

The units are intended to be used in order as the basis of a complete curriculum (once you add in a systematic math, reading, and writing program). You begin with Year 1 Unit 1 no matter what ages your children are. Spend about 2 weeks on each unit. You pick and choose the activities within the unit that appeal to you and read the books from the book list that are available to you or find others on the same topic from your library. We highly recommend that you use the timeline in every history section as the backbone. Then flesh out your learning with reading and activities that highlight the topics you think are the most important.

Alternatively, you can use the units as activity ideas to supplement another curriculum in any order you wish. You can still use them with all ages of children at the same time.

When you've finished with Year One, move on to Year Two, Year Three, and Year Four. Then begin again with Year One and work your way through the years again. Now your children will be older, reading more involved books, and writing more in depth. When you have completed the sequence for the second time, you start again on it for the third and final time. If your student began with Layers of Learning in 1st grade and stayed with it all the way through she would go through the four year rotation three times, firmly cementing the information in her mind in ever increasing depth. At each level you should expect increasing amounts of outside reading and writing. High schoolers in particular should be reading extensively, and if possible, participating in discussion groups.

☺ ☻ ☻ These icons will guide you in spotting activities and books that are appropriate for the age of child you are working with. But if you think an activity is too juvenile or too difficult for your kids, adjust accordingly. The icons are not there as rules, just guides.

☺ GRADES 1-4
☻ GRADES 5-8
☻ GRADES 9-12

Within each unit we share:
- EXPLORATIONS, activities relating to the topic;
- EXPERIMENTS, usually associated with science topics;
- EXPEDITIONS, field trips;
- EXPLANATIONS, teacher helps or educational philosophies.

In the sidebars we also include Additional Layers, Famous Folks, Fabulous Facts, On the Web, and other extra related topics that can take you off on tangents, exploring the world and your interests with a bit more freedom. The curriculum will always be there to pull you back on track when you're ready.

You can learn more about how to use this curriculum at www.layers-of-learning.com/layers-of-learning-program/

UNIT SEVEN

PHOENICIANS – OCEANS – MOTION – MORAL STORIES

When you sell a man a book you don't sell just twelve ounces of paper and ink and glue - you sell him a whole new life. Love and friendship and humour and ships at sea by night - there's all heaven and earth in a book, a real book.
-Christopher Morley

	LIBRARY LIST:
HISTORY	Search for: Phoenicians, Carthage, purple dye, murex shells, Tyre, Sidon, Dido, Hannibal, Punic Wars. This is a hard to find subject, especially when it comes to kids' books. You'll want to rely on your history encyclopedia and information from the internet for most of this unit. ☺ ☻ Hannibal: Rome's Worst Nightmare by Phillip Brooks. From the Horrible Histories Series. ☺ ☻ The Young Carthaginian by G.A. Henty. Fictional history from one of the best storytellers ever. Young boy, great adventures, great moral courage, and a memorable setting in the days of Hannibal.
GEOGRAPHY	Search for: oceans, seashore, coastlines, islands, water cycle, ships ☺ I Wonder Why The Sea Is Salty and Other Questions About the Oceans by Anita Ganeri. ☺ The Magic School Bus On the Ocean Floor by Joanna Cole. From the original series, not a knock-off. Excellent text and illustrations. ☺ Seashore: One Small Square by Donald Silver. Takes the life and environment of one square foot of seashore and describes it in detail, giving a wonderful overall picture of the seashore. ☺ Down Comes The Rain by Franklyn M. Branley. An easy-reader book about the water cycle. ☺ The Little Island by Margaret Wise Brown. Visit an island and its life all through the seasons. The illustrations won a Caldecott Medal. ☺ An Island Grows by Lola M. Schaefer. Traces the formation of an island and life that covers it. Powerful, strong and simple language. ☺ An Island Scrapbook by Virginia Wright-Frierson. A deep look at the ecology of a North Carolina Barrier Island. ☺ ☻ Oceans by Semour Simon. ☺ ☻ Ocean by Miranda MacQuitty. From DK, an "Eyewitness" book. ☺ Coastlines By Michael Kerrigan. Part of the "Geography Fact Files" series. ☺ ☻ ☻ Atlas of Oceans by Linda Sonntag. Covers everything from formation of the ocean floor to human use and economics. Very worthwhile.

SCIENCE	Search for: gravity, friction ☺ Gravity Is a Mystery by Franklyn M. Branley and Edward Miller. An easy reader, this book is particularly excellent because instead of pretending we know all about gravity, the book explains the effects and admits we don't know why or how it works. ☺ Forces Make Things Move by Kimberly Brubaker Bradley. Covers forces, reactions, inertia, friction, and gravity in a scientific and yet kid friendly way. ☺ ☻ Gravity by Janice Van Cleave. A book of experiments relating to gravity. ☻ Force and Motion by Peter Lafferty. A DK Eyewitness book, and in DK style, full of awesome visuals to bring the words to life. ☻ Head First Physics by Heather Lang. Way beyond the basics, this book helps the student to internalize and really understand the physical, mechanical, and mathematical basics of physics in a conversational non-text book format. Requires an understanding of some trigonometric principles. For upper high school.
THE ARTS	Search for: fables, Aesop's Fables, parables, moral stories, moral tales ☺ The Blind Men and The Elephant by Karen Backstein (retold). An old Buddhist parable told in an easy reader picture book. ☺ ☻ The Ugly Duckling by Hans Christian Anderson and Jerry Pinkney. A Caldecott honor book for its beautiful art; this fable is a favorite of children. (If you can't find this version, your library probably has others.) ☺ ☻ The Aesop For Children With Pictures by Milo Winter. This may just be my favorite version of Aesop's Fables because it is so authentic. The illustrations have a beautiful, old-world feel. ☺ ☻ Aesop's Fables. Illustrated by Safaya Salter. This version of the fables is written in condensed, simplified language. Less classic, but very easy to understand. The colorful illustrations are breathtaking and full of charm. ☺ ☻ ☻ Tales of the Dervishes By Idries Shah. A collection of ancient and medieval tales from the Middle East. Excellent read alouds for any age. The tales all have a moral behind them, usually one relating to the way the human mind works and the logical fallacies we all fall into.

HISTORY: PHOENICIANS

Additional Layer

There are very few primary source documents of the Phoenicians. This is partly because many of their records were written on perishable papyrus and partly because all their cities were thoroughly sacked and destroyed. Most of what we know about them has come from records written by their enemies, like the Romans, or from archaeological digs at important city sites and underwater shipwrecks.

Learn more about primary source documents and their importance in understanding history.

The Phoenicians descended from the Canaanites. Their culture really got underway from about 1200 BC onward. They were explorers, artists, and above all, traders. It was a people made mighty through money and a culture that conquered through cash. Phoenicians never were a nation in the modern sense of the word; they were not an empire. Instead, they had many separate city states and small kingdoms sharing a common language and culture. Though they had warships and armies, they were not a warlike people. They conquered instead through trade. Their ships sailed across vast areas on quests to make money. They colonized all over the Mediterranean to promote trade with the locals. At least one lasting piece of their culture has come down to us today: their alphabet, a phonetic (the word comes from Phoenician) use of symbols. Even the symbols we use today are descended from the Phoenicians. On the north coast of Africa they built one of their greatest cities, Carthage, and became known as the Carthaginians. Eventually, they were conquered by Alexander the Great in the east and Rome in the west.

☺ ☺ ☻ EXPLORATION: Phoenician Map
Make a map of the Mediterranean showing the colonies of the Phoenicians. Some of the colonies were as far away as the south coast of Spain and Carthage in Africa. You'll find "The Phoenicians" map in the printables at the end of this unit.

Additional Layer

The city of Tyre, one of the main Phoenician ports, is mentioned several times in the Bible too. See if you can find it.

First, find it on the map. Next, find it in the Bible. If your Bible has a map section in it, you can even find it on a map in the Bible!

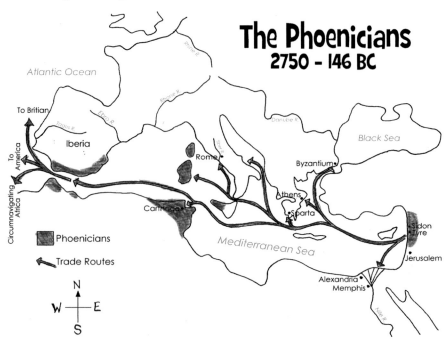

☺ ☺ ☻ EXPLORATION: Timeline

All the dates below are approximate, sometimes nothing more than hearsay or guessing, but it's the best we've got. There is a printable set of timeline squares at the end of this unit.

- 2750 BC Founding of Tyre
- 1500 BC Settlement of Cyprus
- 1300 BC Trade treaties with Egypt
- 1200 BC Tyre becomes foremost of Phoenician cities (concurrent with the Trojan War)
- 1100 BC Cadiz and colonies on the Atlantic coast established
- 980 BC King Hiram makes trade treaties with David and Solomon and sends out trade expeditions
- 876 BC Phoenicians pay tribute to Assyria
- 813 BC Founding of Carthage
- 636 BC Eastern Phoenicians throw off Assyrian rule
- 538 BC Becomes a province of Persia
- 500 BC Hanno circumnavigates Africa
- 332 BC Tyre falls to Alexander the Great, marking the end of the eastern Phoenicians
- 264 BC Carthage begins Punic Wars with Rome
- 218 BC Hannibal crosses the Alps with his army and runs rampant all over Italy
- 201 BC Carthage falls to Rome
- 146 BC End of the Punic Wars and end of western Phoenicians

☺ ☻ EXPLORATION: Famous Folks

Here are a few famous Phoenicians. Look up more information on them. Write an essay explaining who they were, some of their ideas or achievements, and what you think of them.

> Sanchuniathon
> Thales of Miletus
> Pythagoras
> Jezebel
> Zeno of Citium
> Himilco
> Hanno the Navigator

☺ ☻ EXPLORATION: Ivory Carvings

The Phoenicians were known for their ivory carvings. Make your own "ivory" carvings from a bar of white soap. Teach the kids how to safely use a sharp knife. Have them sketch a simple design, or etch it right on to the bar of soap and then carve away the extra bits. Fish, hearts, turtles, trees, flowers, leaves, whales, and faces are all simple shapes to try to carve.

Additional Layer

There are conflicting accounts of whether the Phoenicians practiced religious child sacrifice in order to appease their gods. The accounts stating they did sacrifice children all come from their enemies. No records written by the Phoenicians themselves exist to say one way or the other and the archaeological finds are inconclusive. Many historical fiction novels about the Phoenicians depict child sacrifice.

The Tyrian god Molok with a victim

Fabulous Fact

This is a Phoenician ship's anchor found in the city of Byblos.

Fabulous Fact
Stuff Carthage traded around the Western world:

Tyrinian purple dye, so expensive that high Roman officials could only afford a single stripe of purple on their togas.

Finely embroidered textiles

Pottery, glassware, and precious metals and stone vessels

Incense and perfume

Furniture and household tools

Fine furniture

Atlantic fish, salted down for transport

Commodities crops like wheat and barley

Besides these things they also acted as the middle man in trading between other nations . . . of course making a hefty profit along the way.

Additional Layer
Many people believe the Phoenicians traveled as far as Britain, and even the Americas. They also circumnavigated Africa millennia before the Europeans did it. Read *The Discovery of the Americas* by Betsy and Giulio Maestro for more about these ancient explorations.

☺ ☻ ☻ EXPLORATION: Purple People

Phoenicians were known for their purple dye. In fact the word "Phoenician" comes from a Greek word which means purple men. The purple dye was obtained from a shellfish found in the Mediterranean, called the murex. It was expensive and rare, which is why purple became the color of royalty in Europe. Make a royal pillowcase with purple dye. You could go diving for murex, but we suggest using RIT dye from the supermarket, which is not from shells, but actually from chemicals. Try tie dyeing with rubber bands or using crayon batik.

To do crayon batik, color a design directly on the cloth using crayons. Make sure the wax is nice and thick. Wherever you colored, the dye will not stick. Then dye the cloth according to the directions on the package.

☺ ☻ ☻ EXPLORATION: Phoenician Ships

The Phoenicians were expert sailors and traders with rugged ships. Tyre, Sidon, and Byblos were three of their main cities, primarily because these cities were right on the coast and were perfect trading ports.

To make a model of a Phoenician boat you'll need these things:
- a large banana
- torn newspaper strips
- paper mache paste (combination of flour and water to create a thin paste)
- A wooden skewer
- a 4" x 4" square piece of poster board or card stock (punch 2 holes in it, one at the top center and one at the bottom center
- craft paints

To make the ship, start by covering the banana with strips of newspaper soaked in paper maché paste. Layer the strips on until the bottom half of the banana is covered. Stick the wooden skewer in the top. (You can paper maché the mast too as long as you don't let it get too thick to put the sail on later. Let it dry (may take overnight). Once it's dry, remove the banana and paint the ship. The Phoenicians had wooden ships, so you may want to paint it brown. Once it's dry, slip your sail on over the mast. You can roll the paper gently to give it the right shape before putting it on your ship.

The Phoenicians would have loaded their ships with tin, purple cloth, cedar wood, and glass. Put tiny items on to your boat to represent each of these. You could use a piece of foil, purple cloth or yarn, a toothpick or small piece of wood, and a glass marble.

There is also a Phoenician ship coloring page at the end of this unit in the printables section.

☺ ☻ EXPLORATION: The Canaanites
The Old Testament tells about the Phoenicians, but it calls them "Canaanites." The Israelites wanted to take over the land, so Moses sent spies in to check it out.

Settle down with a snack – get some grapes (and pomegranates and figs if you have them) and read the story from Numbers chapters 13 and 14. It tells about the spies finding grapes and also some of the other things they saw in the land of Canaan.

☺ ☻ EXPLORATION: The Dido Problem
Though not necessarily factual, the Roman poet Virgil told this story in his Aeneid:

A young Phoenician woman named Dido had to flee from her homeland after her brother killed her husband. Her greedy brother was after their riches. She took several boats and quite a few people along with her, and set sail for the African coast. When she arrived, she made a deal with the king there. She would pay him a large sum of money for as much land as she could mark out with the hide of a bull. The king, thinking he was getting a great deal, agreed. After all, how much land could the skin of one bull cover?

Memorization Station
Memorize the BC dates of the Punic Wars.

1st Punic War 264-241
2nd Punic War 218-201
3rd Punic War 149-146

Famous Folks

This is the sarcophagus of King Ahirom of Byblos. It was discovered by French archaeologist Pierre Montet. No other reference to this king of Byblos has ever been found. The artwork carved on the sarcophagus is one of the few examples of Phoenician work of this period.

Fabulous Fact

This is a small two-masted coastal sailing vessel called a corbita. This carving was found at Carthage and is now in the British Museum.

Famous Folks

Dido, also known as Elissa, was raised as a princess in the city of Tyre. She fled the city with some faithful followers when her younger brother became a king and a tyrant (he had a penchant for murdering family members.) Dido then sailed to the north coast of Africa and founded a new colony there. We can't be sure how much of this story is true and how much is legend.

Fabulous Fact

Carthaginians used mercenaries for most of their land-based armies. They also used the now extinct North African elephant in war. Learn about this extinct species of elephant.

Additional Layer

Hannibal's crossing of the Alps has inspired many artists. Look up some of the paintings and drawings done of this event (search for Hannibal Crossing the Alps under "images" online). Compare them. Learn about the artists. Draw or paint your own rendition of Hannibal crossing the Alps.

Each person gets one brown paper bag, cut apart so it lays as one flat piece. This represents the bull skin. Your challenge is to mark out the biggest piece of land you can using the skin. How much can you cover?

Once everyone is finished with the challenge, continue on with the story:

Dido was wiser than the king had thought. She cut the skin into skinny strips, sewed them all together, and marked off a big enough area of land to surround a large hill that she could found the city of Carthage on. Dido became the first queen of Carthage, known for her intellect and mathematical skill.

Dido Building Carthage by Joseph Mallord William Turner (1815)

Isoperimetric problems (which enclose a maximum area inside a fixed boundary) are now commonly known as "Dido problems" among mathematicians.

☺ ☺ ☻ EXPLORATION: The Cedars of Lebanon

The legendary "Cedars of Lebanon" were cedar trees from the Phoenician lands along the eastern edge of the Mediterranean, because timber was so scarce in that region, they were very valuable. Cedar was particularly valuable because its smell, though appealing to people, is not appealing to bugs. This means that buildings built from it are insect resistant and longer lasting. The cedars of Lebanon were traded all over the Mediterranean and used in many important building projects. They were used to build Phoenician ships, buildings, and temples. Solomon's Temple was built from them. When archaeologists opened the tomb of Cheops, the Egyptian pharaoh, some of the artifacts were made of cedar, and still smelled like cedar all those thousands of years later when the tomb was opened.

If you have cedar wood in your home somewhere, sand it down a bit to release the smell. If you don't have any at home visit a lumber store and get a whiff of some cedar. Learn more about why it's such a long-lasting wood.

The cedars of Lebanon were sold and traded so much that they nearly became extinct. Now there is a project underway to restore them. Over 50 million of them are being planted every year in an attempt to reforest the area. Unfortunately, there have been many varieties of trees around the world that have become extinct. It's ridiculous to let this happen because trees are a completely renewable resource. As long as we always plant more than we use, we will never run out. Plant some trees on your property or somewhere in your community. If you join the Arbor Day Foundation they will send you ten trees for $10.00 for you to plant.

Cedar of Lebanon, shared by David Hawgood

☺ ☻ **EXPLORATION: The First Alphabet**
As far as we know, the Phoenicians were the first people to develop a phonetic alphabet rather than a symbolic or pictograph based writing system.

Read *How The First Letter Was Written* and *How the First Alphabet Was Made*, two *Just So Stories* by Rudyard Kipling. They are fictional tales about how letters and the alphabet came to be. *How the First Letter Was Written* may make you think about what it would be like to try to communicate through writing long distances without a phonetic alphabet to rely on. After you've read the tales, then try to write a letter or note to someone without using any phonetic letters. You have to try to get them to do

Definitions
Punic is another word for Phoenician, thus the *Punic* Wars with Rome.

"Carthage" means new city, as in Tyre renewed. We'd probably call it "New Tyre."

Carthage Ruins

Fabulous Fact
The Phoenicians worshiped many gods including Tanit, Baal, Astarte, and other gods borrowed from the Greeks and others. But there were also colonies of Jews within all their cities, including Carthage. The descendants of the Carthaginian Jews still live there in modern day Tunisia.

Fabulous Fact
Carthaginian slave traders took conquered northern Europeans to Africa to be traded into slavery.

Teaching Tip

Simulated letters are great learning tools because they help kids imagine themselves at a place and time in history. They put themselves in the shoes of someone else and write a letter about what they're experiencing. If this is difficult at first, give them a start by helping them think of the 5 W's (When did they live? What are they doing? Why? Who are they with? Where are they?) Help them visualize what it might have really been like by describing their surroundings, then let them write the letter.

Rather than correcting it, let their feedback be a letter in response. Write a letter back to them from whoever the original letter was addressed to.

Fabulous Fact

Phoenician traders and merchants invented auction sales. . .

who'llgivemetwenty, twentyanyone-givemetwentycomeon-givemetwenty

something only by using pictures you've drawn (like take the garbage out or fix you a snack). Can you do it?

☺ ☻ ☻ EXPLORATION: Phoenician Alphabet

Because the Phoenicians were traders, they did a lot of traveling. Why do you think it would have been important to them to have an alphabet?

Pretend you are a Phoenician on a long voyage at sea. Write a letter home to your family telling them about your travels, the sights you're seeing, and the people you're meeting along the way.

☺ ☻ ☻ EXPLORATION: Now I Know My ABC's

There are many similarities between our modern alphabet and the Phoenician alphabet. Why do you think this is so? on the chart at the end of this unit, highlight or color the letters that you can see similarities between. Then use the Phoenician letters to write a note to someone.

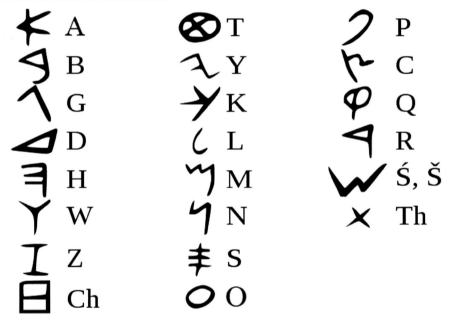

☺ ☻ EXPLORATION: The Siege of Tyre

Alexander the Great arrived at the city of Tyre in 333 BC. The people of the city had, of course, heard that he was on his way. They abandoned the portion of the city that was on the mainland, sent their women and children away to Carthage, and retreated into their island fortress, just off the coast. Alexander was therefore prevented from using his siege engines and had to instead surround and blockade the city for seven months. During that time, his soldiers amused themselves by tearing down buildings and walls from the mainland city of Tyre.
Alexander had the bright idea of building a causeway from the

rubble, extending toward the island though the sea. Once it had reached far enough, Alexander rolled his siege engines out on the rampart and began to bombard the walls. The Tyrians fought back, sending fire ships at the siege engines and destroying them. Eventually

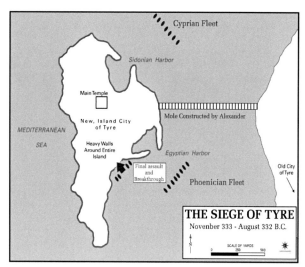

THE SIEGE OF TYRE
November 333 - August 332 B.C.

Alexander obtained a navy, mounted siege engines on the boats, destroyed a portion of the walls, and took his men in by boat through the breach. Alexander was so ticked off with the city for causing him so much trouble that he killed or enslaved the entire population, except the king of Tyre, who he forgave.

This was the end of the Phoenician civilization in the East. But Alexander's causeway is still there, silted up and forming a land bridge to the former island.

Choose one of these activities to go along with your study of the Siege of Tyre.

- Paint or draw (ink drawings filled in with watercolor come out very professional looking) a dramatic scene from the siege, like the fire ships burning the siege engines.
- Research and reconstruct a model of what Alexander's siege engines looked like.
- Write an "eye-witness" account of the battle. You could be either a Tyrian or a Macedonian (Alexander's army).
- Make a detailed timeline of the siege.
- Use a 9" x 13" pan and create a diorama of the scene, complete with the causeway. Use the map above as a reference.
- Study one of the episodes of the battle, like the building of the causeway, which in the end was useless, and analyze what mistakes and triumphs each side made.
- Reenact a part of the battle.

☺ ☺ ☺ EXPLORATION: Hannibal the Hero

Hannibal was a wildly successful general in the waning days of Carthage during the second Punic War. He's famous for, first, taking all of Spain from the Romans, thus violating the treaty

Ruins From the City of Tyre

Triumphal arch from Tyre.
Photograph by David Bjorgen.

Fabulous Fact

This is a Phoenician coin. This particular coin was from the city of Tyre. It was found in a treasure horde with other coins, but this was the only Phoenician one.

Additional Layer

Aristotle's book, Politics, discusses the Carthaginian constitution in book II, chapter 11.

Fabulous Fact

This is a drawing of ruins of the city of Tyre. It was destroyed repeatedly.

Fabulous Fact

The Phoenicians were the best sailors in the world during their day. They cleaned up on the Romans in sea battles until the Romans stole some of their boats and figured out the Phoenician secrets.

Hannibal ad Portus!

For centuries after Hannibal ransacked the Roman countryside the people of Rome remembered the terror he had caused. Whenever destruction in any form threatened they would cry,"Hannibal ad Portus!" which means *Hannibal is at the gates*, or in other words, we're doomed. Sometimes people still use this phrase when referring to imminent calamity coming upon them.

with Rome and plunging the Carthaginians into the second Punic War. Second, he led his army, including a great many elephants, overland (Rome was a terror on the seas by this point) across the Alps. "Barbarian" tribes living in the Alps made his life not worth living for several months, but Hannibal pushed on into Italy where he trounced the Romans who then hardly dared to step out of their fortified capital of Rome lest Hannibal be waiting. Hannibal tromped up and down the countryside at will, until finally a Roman general got permission from the senate and beat Hannibal, who fled the peninsula. Eventually the Romans caught up with Hannibal again in Anatolia and the Levant where he was advising and commanding Seleucid troops who were resisting the Romans. Threatened and on the defensive, the Seleucid king had agreed to give Hannibal to the Romans. Rather than be subjected to this indignity, Hannibal took poison and died.

You really must learn much more about this amazing and fascinating man, called one of the greatest generals of all time. In particular I think you'll enjoy the story of Hannibal attacking using snakes . . . or how about the time he swore eternal hatred of the Romans when just a child . . . or the time Hannibal was nearly caught and destroyed against the banks of the Rhone River . . . but I wouldn't want to spoil it for you.

GEOGRAPHY: OCEANS

Oceans cover about 71% of the surface of the earth. They are essential to life on Earth as they are the source of most of our oxygen, much of our food, all of our water, and our mild temperatures. Without the huge oceans Earth would not be nearly so nice. There is really just one huge body of water we call ocean, but we divide them up for our own convenience and give them names: Pacific Ocean, Atlantic Ocean, Indian Ocean, Arctic Ocean, and Southern Ocean.

Photograph by Sean O'Flaherty

In this unit we'll learn about the water cycle, life in the oceans, human activity in and on the oceans, the geography of the land below the surface, the effect the oceans have on worldwide climates, and some of the geology of the oceans.

☺ ☻ **EXPLORATION: Ocean in a Bottle**
Use this project to kick off your oceans unit.

You need:
- an empty 2 liter plastic bottle with a lid
- clear cooking oil or mineral spirits
- water
- a funnel
- blue food coloring

Additional Layer

Read Eric Carle's *Mister Seahorse* and discuss 1) how and why some species use camouflage, and 2) the species of fish that have their fathers rather than their mothers care for them.

Additional Layer

When oil spills happen within our oceans, they leave disastrous messes that are difficult to clean up and can harm plant and animal life in the area they spilled. To keep things in perspective though, more oil reaches the oceans each year in little bits from leaking automobiles and things than has ever spilled off an oil tanker. When tankers leak it looks dramatic because it's all in one place, but there are bits of oil being dripped in from other sources far more.

Even more interesting is that oil naturally escapes from vents in the ocean floor in far greater quantities than any disaster. Look up the numbers and create a graph showing where the oil in the oceans comes from.

Additional Layer
Within our own little ocean bottle, the oil and water don't mix because the hydrogen bonds in the water are strong. The oil bonds are not strong enough to break the water's hydrogen bonds, so the two liquids can't combine. The oil is less dense than the water, so it stays above it and allows us to see the wave action when we tip the bottle back and forth.

Additional Layer
Bathymetry is the study of underwater topography.

Image from NOAA.

On the Web

Check out our ocean Pinterest board for fun ocean crafts.
http://www.pinterest.com/layerslearning/ocean-unit/

1. First, fill the bottle halfway with water. Add a few drops of blue food coloring and swirl it around until it mixes.

2. Using a funnel, add oil or mineral spirits up to the top of the bottle. Put the lid on tightly. (You may want to put a little hot glue around the rim if you're worried about it leaking.)

3. Now rock the bottle on it's side gently to create a wave that goes back and forth.

If you want to, you may add small shells, sand, or tiny fish-shaped beads before sealing the bottle.

Interesting tidbits to discuss:

- Water covers 71 percent of the world's surface.
- If you could weigh ocean water it would weigh 1.45 trillion tons!!
- There are over 1 million species of known marine animals that live there, and many more yet to be discovered. Some scientists guess there may be as many as 9 million more we haven't discovered yet!
- The ocean floor is covered with ridges, mountain ranges, and canyons.
- The blue whale is the largest mammal on the earth and has a heart the size of a Volkswagen.
- The Great Barrier Reef is 1,243 miles and is the largest living structure on Earth. You can see it from space.
- The ocean is like a treasure chest. It contains not only valuable minerals, but also spices (like salt), fish and other marine life that we eat, and oil that we depend on for fuel.
- Learn about salinity and properties of sea water.

☺ ☻ **EXPERIMENT: Water Cycle**
The water you drank today has been on Earth as water since the beginning of time . . . just in case you thought it was fresh. It does get a regular cleaning and recycling though through something called the water cycle. Water collects in the oceans, where it evaporates, filling the air with moisture. When enough moisture has collected the water vapor makes clouds. When the clouds become saturated enough the water falls as rain. The rain washes the sky and cleans the surfaces on Earth. Then the rain water filters though the soil rock, getting really clean. Eventually it all

comes up to the surface again where it collects in streams and lakes and runs back to the ocean and we start all over again.

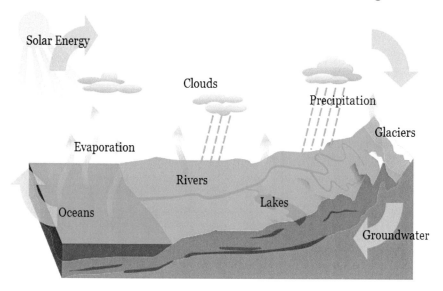

Make a terrarium to show the water cycle. You need a large bottle. If you want a really cool big glass jar, like this one, go ask at a restaurant if they have something left over. Add soil, a few plants, a dish of water, and water the soil well. Then cover the whole thing with plastic wrap, held on firmly with a rubber band. In the center of the plastic wrap set a rock, to weight down the center. The moisture in your terrarium will evaporate and collect on the walls and "roof" of the bottle. It will then drip down back into the soil, like rain. As long as you keep it covered, the terrarium will last a long time with no care required.

Experiment with different conditions. What if your terrarium is kept cool? What if it is placed in direct sunlight? What if you place it in partial sunlight? How do these things change the rate of the water cycle?

Make a poster board with a diagram of the water cycle and describe your experiment with the terrarium.

Teaching Tip

As you begin to teach about water and oceans, hold a freshly poured glass of ice water up and ask, "How old do you think this water is?"

Hopefully that should spark some discussion about how water cycles around and around. Just because we drink it, water our flowers, or let it run down the sink doesn't mean it's gone.

Teaching Tip

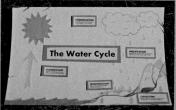

To create our water cycle poster I printed out the words ahead of time, and then had the kids take turns drawing the parts and gluing on the word strips. Once you've created your poster let each kid take a turn describing the cycle all the way around. Let them put on the teacher's hat for a few minutes.

Karen

Additional Layer
Draw a simple food chain showing how animals within a small region depend on each other for food.

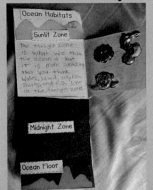

Make a pamphlet with the ocean zones labeled on the outside and a description inside.

☺ ☻ EXPLORATION: Ocean Zones

Different areas of the oceans have different names and support different forms of life. The major ocean zones are named according to the amount of light that penetrates. They are:

1. The sunlight zone
2. The twilight zone
3. The midnight zone
4. The abyss
5. The trenches

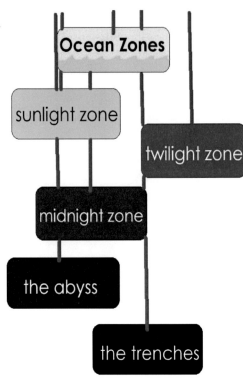

Make a mobile showing the different levels of the ocean zones. The sunlit zone will be at the top and the trenches at the bottom. You can include pictures of animals, plants, and microorganisms found at each layer.

☺ ☻ EXPLORATION: Trenches, Shelves, Ridges, and Mounts

At the end of this unit you'll find a blank outline map of the world. On this map label the major ocean trenches, shelves, ridges, and undersea mounts in the world oceans. Your student atlas should have a physical map of Earth showing some of the major oceanic formations. But before you label the map you need to know what each of these things is.

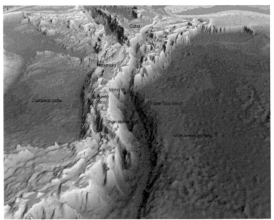

The deepest trench in the Atlantic Ocean, between the Caribbean Sea and the Atlantic. Image by USGS.

Ocean trenches are places in the Earth's crust where one crustal plate is sinking under another. Where they meet, a deep crease is formed. The oceanic trenches are the deepest places on Earth. The deepest point we know of on Earth is called Challenger Deep and is in the Mariana Trench in the Pacific Ocean.

Shelves are where the continental plates rise from the deeper, thinner oceanic plates. The shelves are where human activity is mostly concentrated and where the fish we like to eat are mostly found, because this is much shallower, warmer water. Along the edge of every continent is a continental shelf. We won't actually label these on the map.

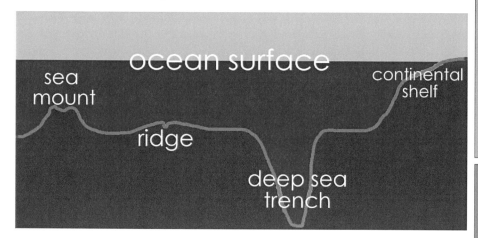

Ridges are long, raised areas where two oceanic plates are pulling away from each other. In the center where they divide, magma wells up, creating new land.

Sea mounts are formed where hot spots under the ocean crust make undersea volcanoes or where ridges are pushed up high enough to form mountain ranges. When they have grown enough, they form islands. The Hawaiian Islands are examples of hot spot sea mounts. But on the map you'll label just a few of the sea mounts that have not yet broken through the surface. Sea Mounts are some of the least understood, under mapped, and dangerous formations on the sea floor. They have caused many shipwrecks and submarine collisions. In addition, when there are underwater landslides they have the potential to create huge tsunami waves.

Additional Layer
Learn about the deepest ever exploration performed by the *Bathyscaphe Trieste* which descended to the bottom of Challenger Deep, the deepest known part of the ocean in the Mariana Trench near Guam.

Items to color and label:

Mariana Trench
Aleutian Trench
Tonga Trench
Middle America Trench
Peru-Chile Trench
Puerto Rico Trench
Mid-Atlantic Ridge

Southwest Indian Ridge
Mid-Indian Ridge
Louisville Ridge
Emperor Sea Mounts
Mid-Pacific Mountains
Nazca Ridge

Teaching Tip
There are quite a few cool ocean maps to make in this unit. You could combine them into one map to get an overall view of the Earth's oceans – currents, topography, resources, and all.

Additional Layer

Not only did we not know until recently what was on the sea floor, we really didn't care. But the advent of cross-oceanic telegraph cables and then later submarine warfare meant humans had an interest. Learn about the laying of the first trans-Atlantic cable and the myriad of experimentation and trial and error that had to be performed before it was possible.

Additional Layer

Find out about some jobs people do that have to do with the ocean. Explore everything from marine biologists to cruise ship operators.

Expedition

If you have the chance, go to a rocky shore and explore the tide pools, the area of the shore which is underwater during the high tide and exposed at low tide. These tide pools are filled with interesting sea life.

😊 😊 😊 **EXPERIMENT: Currents**

A current is a slow steady flow of a fluid. Ocean currents are the flow of water around the globe. Currents are caused by various factors. Currents on the surface are often caused by the prevailing winds, which are caused, in turn, by the rotation of the earth. Deep sea currents are caused by differences in the salinity and temperature of water in the ocean. Surface water tends to be more saline than deeper ocean water, because it is from the surface that water is evaporating and leaving behind more salts. Sea surface temperatures and sea temperatures near the equator are much warmer than deep sea temperatures and temperatures near the poles. These temperature differentials cause water to flow in currents as well. Besides this, the effect of tides and the shape of continental shorelines have a big effect on currents.

To see how salinity affects the flow of water try this experiment. Get two small jars of water. In one dissolve as much salt as you can and add a couple of drops of blue food coloring. In the second jar leave it fresh water and add red food coloring. Place a piece of card stock or an index card over the opening of the salty jar. Invert it onto the other jar and carefully remove the card. Observe how the two waters, salty and not salty interact with each other.

Repeat the experiment using hot and cold water instead of salty and fresh.

😊 😊 😊 **EXPLORATION: Current Map**

Oceans and their currents drastically affect the climate of Earth. The classic example is the mild weather of high northern latitudes of Europe due to the gulf stream. Look at a world map to see which North American cities are on the same latitude as European cities and compare the climates.

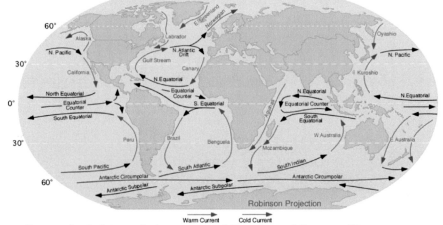

At the end of this unit is a printable of world prevailing ocean currents. Color it.

☺ ☻ EXPLORATION: Tides

Tides are the overall rising and falling of sea levels at the shore. They are caused by a combination of the gravitational pull of the moon and the sun and the rotation of the earth.

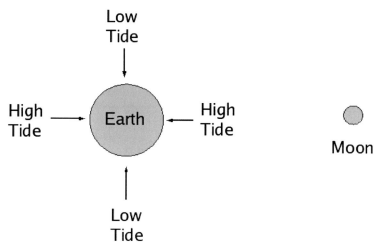

Image created by Jim Thomas

Most places have two high and two low tides in a day, but some places have only one set of tides. Some places have very dramatic tides, while others vary by only a few feet. The shape of the shoreline and the topography of the sea bed near the shore are the largest factors in determining how dramatic the tide in a certain place will be. Tides in a particular place can be higher or lower at certain seasons of the year depending on the positions of the sun and moon. Forecasting the time and amplitude of tides is a complicated science.

Make a diagram of how the moon is involved in high and low tides as seen above or use the world map at the end of this unit and trace the outlines of the world's shores showing whether they have semi-diurnal (once daily) or diurnal (twice daily) or mixed tides as seen on the following map.

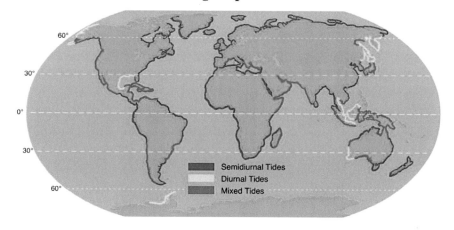

Explanation

Any parent who wants to supplement their child's education can do a once a week method of teaching. Once my two oldest and I spent more than six months doing drawing lessons from a How-to-draw course. The kids didn't even realize it was a "school" subject.

Here are some things to consider doing one evening a week:

-Art projects or courses
-Nature projects
-Star gazing and identifying constellations
-Any type of science projects
-Reading books together
-Book projects
-History crafts or activities
-Math games (like Sum Swamp)
-Educational trivia games (I really like the Professor Noggin series)
-Cooking together
-Learning a musical instrument, like the piano, guitar, or recorder.
-Doing projects from different countries or cultures around the world
-Think of more based on your child's interests

Michelle

Deep Question

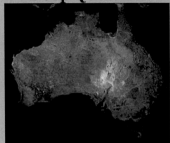

Is Australia a really big island or a continent? What makes a continent a continent? There is no accepted absolute size standard.

Writer's Workshop

Pretend you have spent the afternoon scuba diving on a coral reef. You don't want to forget one bit of the experience. Write about all that you saw and did as a simulated journal entry.

Additional Layer

People use coral reefs for recreation and fishing around the world. The economic value of the reefs is about $375 billion per year in U.S. dollars. Even though coral reefs have huge economic value, they are endangered in many parts of the world. Ocean pollution, over harvesting of tropical fish and coral, careless behavior of divers and shipping, plus some natural phenomenon kill off huge swaths of reefs.

☺ ☻ EXPLORATION: Reef Diorama

A reef is a rock, sandbar, or biotic growth that is shallow enough for it to be a danger to ships. The type of reef most people think of is a coral reef, made up of tiny sea creatures which grow in colonies until they form huge structures. Coral reefs only thrive in warm shallow waters, but other types of reefs can be found anywhere in the oceans.

Make a coral reef diorama in a shoebox. Begin by painting the background blue. Then paint the lower part of the back and the "floor" orange, yellow, and purple tones using a sponge for texture. Finally, add in drawings of sea creatures that are found on or near coral reefs.

Some of the larger coral reefs on Earth are: Great Barrier Reef, Mesoamerican Barrier Reef System, New Caledonia Barrier Reef, Andros Bahamas Barrier Reef, Red Sea fringing reefs, Pulley Ridge, Maldives reef system, and the Raja Ampat Islands reefs. See if you can find these locations on a map.

☺ ☻ EXPLORATION: Trade on the Ocean

The oceans have been instrumental to trade since the most ancient of times. Today, huge ocean container ships, tankers, and barges ply the shipping lanes of the world carrying on trade between countries. Certain areas of the oceans have been designated as shipping lanes in order to reduce accidents between ships at sea. The shipping lanes are chosen as direct paths between two points but also because of prevailing currents and winds and to avoid dangerous shoals and reefs.

Draw the main shipping routes on the printable "Sea Trade Routes" map from the end of this unit. The thicker lines indicate greater volumes of sea trade.

Sea Trade Routes

☺ ☺ ☺ **EXPLORATION: Resources From the Ocean**

Humans collect an impressive range of natural resources from the ocean. These resources are vital to our economy and well being. From fish for eating to kelp for toothpaste, we depend on the oceans for a whole lot of our stuff. Make a collage poster showing some of the resources we obtain from the ocean. You can draw pictures, cut them from magazines, or find images from the internet to print out. Caption each picture with some facts about the resource. Here is a list to get you started:

fish and shellfish for eating (more than 200 billion pounds a year)
transportation for cargo and leisure
recreation and tourism
crude oil drilling

salt	copper
sand	nickle
gravel	manganese
cobalt	tropical fish as pets

On the Web

Check out the NOAA.gov website for tons of educational online games and activities for kids all relating to the oceans.

Fabulous Fact

The majority of the planet is covered by oceans, so it's not really surprising that a majority of life on Earth is aquatic. About 94% of animals live under the water.

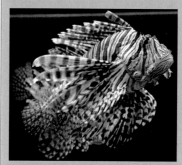

Fabulous Fact

In 1983 President Ronald Reagan of the U.S. declared exclusive rights of all mineral, oil, and other natural resources in the waters up to 200 miles off the coast of the United States. In 1994 this Exclusive Economic Zone (EEZ) rule became internationally recognized law of the seas for all nations.

Additional Layer

Ocean currents of the world collect floating stuff, and eventually all the floaties collect in a few places in the middle of the oceans. These places are called gyres. One gyre in the North Pacific has collected in an area estimated to be twice the size of the state of Texas. What are all these "floaties"? Mostly plastic stuff washed out to sea or purposely dumped there by us.

Read the fabulous book *Tracking Trash: Flotsam, Jetsom, and the Science of Ocean Motion* by Loree Burns to learn more about ocean currents and the trash we dump.

Fabulous Fact

Charles Darwin was the first to observe and postulate on the origin of atolls. It was his theory that the coral rings formed around volcanoes which later sunk, leaving only the ring of coral. His ideas have been borne out by subsequent study.

☻ EXPLORATION: Off-Shore Drilling

The crust under the oceans is much thinner than the continental crust, making it an ideal site for drilling for gas and oil. Known reserves of oil and gas have been found along nearly every coast of every continent all over the world. Oil and gas naturally leak from vents in the ocean floor all the time.

Research and then color a world map (make a copy from the end of this unit) showing the known offshore oil deposits and the major areas of drilling in the ocean.

☻ ☻ EXPLORATION: Islands and Archipelagos

Most islands in the ocean were formed as a result of volcanoes growing up from the sea floor. Even many islands that are built of coral sand got their start as volcanoes, with coral colonies growing on the submerged sides of a volcano and the volcano itself subsiding over time. Since the Earth's crust moves about over the hot magma underneath, archipelagos of islands often form as the crust floats over a hot spot. Alternately, a string of islands can form along the margin of a plate. Many of the islands of the eastern Pacific were formed this way.

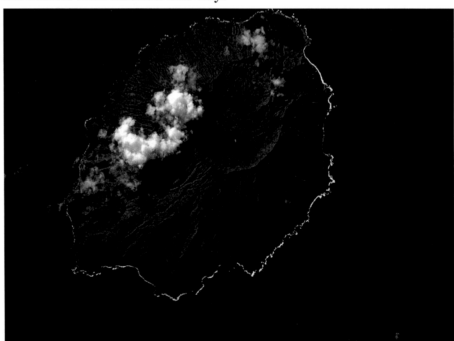

Agrihan Island, Northern Mariana Islands, NASA

Read some books on islands and then make this yummy island snack. Give each child a shallow bowl of blue Jello, previously prepared. Then have them form islands and atolls and archipelagos out of graham crackers, cookies, mini marshmallows, chocolate chips, and so on (raid your cupboards). Talk about their island formations and then let them eat them up.

Talk about the different island formations. Also, here are some definitions to discuss while making your treats:

Atoll: a ring shaped island with a lagoon of sea water in the center.

Archipelago: a group of islands.

Barrier Reef: a type of reef that runs along a coast for some distance.

Cay: a low-lying sandy isle built on top of a coral reef.

Desert Island: a deserted island, without people, not indicating a desert.

Fringing Reef: A reef that runs very nearby a shore and only has a shallow lagoon or no lagoon at all.

Volcanic Island

Fringing Reef

Barrier Reef

Atoll Formation diagram, USGS

☹ ☺ EXPLORATION: Coastal Formations

Geography is more concerned with naming and defining and locating coastal formations than in describing how they formed so we'll save the hows for Earth Science in later units. For now, focus on helping kids recognize what these formations are and some of the places you can find them.

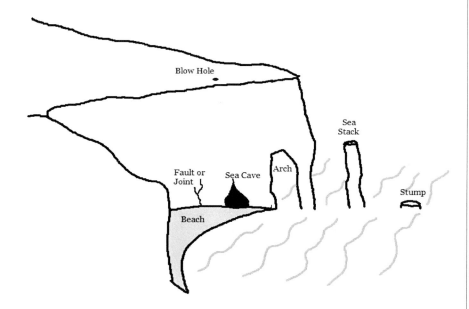

Additional Layer
Harry Potter and the Half Blood Prince and *Over Sea Under Stone* are two books where sea shore formations play a big role.

Fabulous Fact
Concepts like coastal formations and other landforms are both science and geography. Geography is part science, part sociology, and part art.

Fabulous Fact
- Another name for sea cave is littoral cave. Littoral caves are not always on the sea coast. Any cave that was formed by the sea in the past is a littoral cave. Learn about the littoral caves in Norway that are now more than 100 feet from the coast.

-

Photo by Bernard Bradley and shared under cc license.

Draw or label your own diagram of sea formations. You can find a coastal Formations worksheet in the printables of www.Layers-of-Learning.com and at the end of this unit.

☺ ☺ ☻ EXPLORATION: Coastal Features Map
On a blank outline map of Europe from the end of this unit, label these coastal features:
- cape
- isthmus
- strait
- bay
- harbor
- gulf
- headland

☺ ☻ EXPLORATION: Sea and Coast Crossword Puzzle
Print out the Sea and Coast crossword puzzle worksheet found at the end of this unit to help kids work on the definitions of sea features.

Answers: <u>Across</u> *(1) gulf (3) cove (5) headland (6) isthmus (9) ocean (11) bay* <u>Down</u> *(2) fjord (4) peninsula (7) harbor (8) sea (10) cape*

☺ ☻ EXPLORATION: I'm A Headland
Here's a funny song to help you remember what a headland is: (Sing it to the tune of "Oh My Darlin' Clementine.")

I'm a headland, I'm a headland
I'm a headland, yes I am
Sitting high above the ocean
I'm a headland, yes I am.

Got a light house, got a light house,
Got a light house right here.
Right here I've got a light house.
Got a light house right here.

See for miles, See for miles,
See for miles from the top.
See for miles, see for miles,
See for miles from the top

I'm a headland, I'm a headland,
I'm a headland, yes I am.
Sitting high above the ocean,
I'm a headland, yes I am.

☻ ☻ **EXPLORATION: Famous Headlands**

Use the index of a student atlas to find some of these famous headlands:

- Cape of Good Hope, South Africa
- Cape Blanc, Mauritania
- Land's End, Cornwall
- North Cape, Norway (furthest point north)
- Gibraltar
- Kanyakumari, India
- Cape Dezhnev, Russia (eastern point)
- Marin Headlands, California
- Cape Canaveral, Florida
- Cape Fear, North Carolina
- Cape Horn, Chili
- Cape York, Australia
- Diamond Head, Oahu, Hawaii

Harrison Point Lighthouse, Barbados
Photograph by Postdlf

☻ ☻ **EXPLORATION: Lighthouses**

Make a model lighthouse. Use a tall plastic container, like a cottage cheese container as the base. Turn it upside down and cover it with construction paper. Look up some real lighthouses to see how they are designed and which colors to use. For the light on top, attach a small yogurt container, covered in paper as well and painted or drawn on. Why do you think a lighthouse would be placed on a headland or promontory of a rocky coast?

☻ ☻ ☻ **EXPEDITION: A Trip to the Sea**

Take a trip to the ocean to see it first hand. Do this toward the end of your unit so the kids will have all that information fresh in their heads when they see it in real life. Make a point to visit some places along the sea that help them understand the things you've learned, like tide pools, a harbor, and so on.

Lobito Lighthouse, Angola
Photo by Claus Bunks

☻ ☻ ☻ **EXPLORATION: Ocean Animal Report**

Have each child choose a marine animal. Compile a list of questions or information to find out about the animal. Head to the library to find books about their animal on their reading level. Next, direct them to some good websites for even more information. National Geographic's Creature Features are an excellent web resource.

Encourage them to take notes and write down interesting facts as they peruse their books. Depending on their age and abilities, outline the length and expectations, then have them write an animal report about their chosen marine animal.

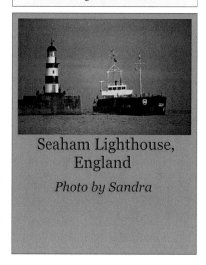

Seaham Lighthouse, England
Photo by Sandra

☺ ☺ ☺ EXPLORATION: Ocean Floor

Create your own ocean floor. Mix cornstarch, sand, and water together in a big pot. Let it come to boil. Once it cools a bit kids can use the messy dough to shape formations like valleys and sea arches in their own ocean floor.

☺ ☺ EXPLORATION: An Ocean of Information

Start with a large piece of blue butcher paper attached to a wall. Have each kid choose between 3 and 10 things that are found under the ocean and that they want to add to an ocean mural. This could be anything from sharks to kelp to dumped garbage. Someone could be responsible for drawing the sea floor. You could also include things that are on the surface, like boats or buoys. Draw a picture and write a small caption describing each item. Once all the items are drawn, cut out, and glued on, you'll have your own ocean of information on the mural.

☺ ☺ ☺ EXPLORATION: Manatees

One of the most interesting ocean animals I've directly encountered are manatees. While living in Florida I visited a rescue area for manatees and also got to swim with some in the wild. Try to find out the only predator of manatees.

There are a lot of animals in the sea that aren't fish. Choose one of these to learn about and make a project for. Have you encountered any marine life first hand?

Karen's husband and daughter touching a manatee

☺ ☺ ☺ EXPEDITION: Aquarium

If possible, take an expedition to an aquarium to see lots of marine life, both plant and animal. Take time to observe the animals, read about them, and become more acquainted with the life that fills our oceans. If you can't get to an aquarium, at least go to a pet store to see some saltwater fish. Find out what is required to care for marine fish.

Karen's kids petting a stingray at the Living Planet Aquarium

SCIENCE: MOTION

Did you know that no one really knows what gravity is? We know what it does, but what is it? Einstein had some theories where he thought gravity was actually the bending of space. But what is space made of? Is it emptiness or is it "stuff"? Einstein thought it was some kind of stuff, but never answered what exactly. One of the most fascinating things about science is that for every discovery or observation thousands of new questions pop up.

Even though we can't pinpoint what it is, we can see how things move due to gravity, circular motion, and friction. We can observe that things always behave in the same ways all the time. There are no exceptions to the laws of the universe. Every single time you throw a ball in the air it will come back down to the ground at some point. Never does a ball just float several feet off the ground or continue into space when thrown by a human arm. There was a manhole cover that is believed to have flown off into space, but that's another subject. Curious? Google it!

☺ ☺ ☺ EXPERIMENT: Which Hits First?

Everything falls at the same rate regardless of its mass. Try it. Drop a medium heavy rock and a piece of paper simultaneously off a high place, like the tree fort or from the top of a ladder. Which hits the ground first? Did the paper fall much slower? Now crinkle up the paper into a ball and try it again. This time which hit the ground first?

Galileo was the first to describe this phenomenon; before that people assumed that lighter things fell more slowly.

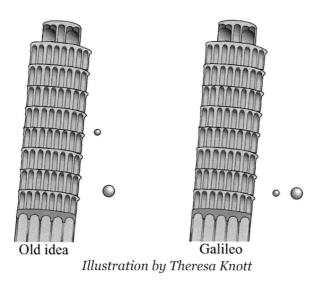

Old idea   Galileo
Illustration by Theresa Knott

Famous Folks

Albert Einstein was smart. Really, really smart. He turned all the old ideas of how motion and gravity work on their heads. He is known as the father of modern physics. And he also had crazy hair, which is fun.

Fabulous Fact

The gravity at Hudson's Bay, Canada is a little lower than at other places on Earth. Scientists think this is because at one time there were huge glaciers sitting in this spot, which pushed into the Earth's crust creating a depression, which has still not rebounded. Since there is less "stuff" in the depression, this makes for less mass. And gravity is directly proportional to mass.

Additional Layer

You probably never think about gravity, but if you were an astronaut you would. It can be as hard for astronauts to adjust to having gravity back as it was to lose it. What problems do you think you might have if you went suddenly from no gravity to normal gravity again?

Additional Layer

NASA has developed an experiment to test whether Einstein's ideas about gravity in the universe can be proved. The experiment is conducted with the help of space probes called Gravity Probe A and B.

On The Web

Look up You Tube videos about gravity for your kids to watch.

Our favorite is *Schoolhouse Rock: Victim of Gravity.*

The first time the spread piece of paper was experiencing friction from the air and the air slowed it down, but the second time the two objects should have hit at the same time even though one weighs much more than the other. Watch Neil Armstrong perform this experiment on the atmosphere-free moon with a feather and a hammer in a You Tube video. Search for "Galileo Experiment" on You Tube. You'll also find a coloring page of the picture from this exploration in the printables section.

☺ ☺ ☻ EXPLORATION: Center of Gravity

Every object has a perfectly balanced point at which gravity has an equal effect. You can find the center of gravity of an irregular shaped piece of tag board. First cut out shape from thick poster board or cereal box cardboard. Then hang a weighted string from one point of the cardboard, let dangle toward the ground. Draw a line recording where the string passes. Repeat with one more point on the cardboard. The spot where the lines cross is the center of gravity. Try balancing your cardboard on a pencil from this point.

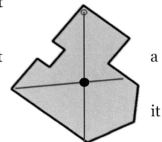

To see how a center of gravity can change with different weights, try balancing a long yard stick off one finger. Then add a lump of clay to some point along the yardstick. How does the center of gravity change? Where do you balance the yard stick from now?

☺ ☺ EXPERIMENT: Human Center of Gravity

Your body has a center of gravity too. When you walk, run, bend, tumble, do a cartwheel, or pick something up off the floor you automatically compensate and adjust your center of gravity so you don't fall over. It wasn't always automatic. Watch a baby learning to walk; it's all about discovering that center of gravity. Try these experiments:

- Face a wall, placing a chair between you and the wall. Bend over, keeping both knees locked, pick up the chair, and then stand up. Girls can do it, but boys cannot. The center of gravity in females is lower, around the hips, than it is for boys.
- Stand with your back flat against the wall, heels to the wall. Place a coin on the ground in front of you. Pick up the coin without moving away from the wall. You can't do it because when people bend over, they scoot their bottoms out to counterbalance the top of their bodies.
- Walk a narrow balance beam with your hands flat against your sides. Try again, using your arms spread out to help balance you. The extended arms keep your center of gravity in

the right place.

- Stand sideways right next to a wall. Try to lift your outside leg straight away from the wall. You can't because normally when you do this move, you balance your body by leaning away from the extending leg.
- Put on a heavy backpack. Try placing it in different spots. Which is easiest to carry? For boys it will be high and on the back. For girls it will be low and on the front. The trick is to put the weight as close to the natural center of gravity as possible.
- Sit in a chair, flat against a wall, facing away from the wall. Have a second person place their thumb on the forehead of the sitting person, to keep their head back against the wall. Now ask the sitter to stand up. You can't, because your center of gravity demands that you lean forward to stand.

☺ ☻ EXPERIMENT: Heavyweight Champ

Find a heavy weight, like a weight belt for exercising. Try to lift it. It should be pretty difficult to lift. Now attach it to a short rope, about 4 feet or less. Now swing it around in a circle. Does it lift off the ground more easily? You swing another child around by their arms this way and lift them off the ground as well. Circular motion makes things easier to lift.

☺ ☺ ☻ EXPERIMENT: Spinning Forces

Can you tip a full cup of water on its side without spilling a drop? You can if you spin it fast enough. Design an experiment with a spinning paper cup of water on a string showing how centrifugal

Writer's Notebook
What would a world without friction be like? Could you walk with nothing to push against? If you were moving, how could you stop? Could you get moving again? (Think Newton's first law!) Think through what a frictionless day would be like and write about it in your writer's notebook. Would you want to live in a world like that?

Additional Layer
Weight and mass aren't the same because mass is a measure of the amount of "stuff" you are made of, but weight depends on the gravity where you happen to be in addition to your mass.

Scale at the Clark Planetarium that tells you how much you'd weigh on other planets given their relative gravity.

Additional Layer
Some injuries, such as rug burns or blisters are caused by friction. Learn how to avoid or treat these kinds of injuries.

force pulls the water outward and centripetal force pulls the string inward.

EXPLANATION: Centrifugal versus Centripetal
Centrifugal force is a circular force pulling outward. Centripetal force is a circular motion being pulled inward. The space shuttle in orbit experiences centripetal force when it flies in a circle around the earth, held there by gravity instead of flying off into space. Gravity acts like a string holding the space shuttle in position.

☺ ☺ ☻ EXPERIMENT: Strong Forces
Get an empty thread spool or another similar cylinder. Thread some fishing line through the cylinder and attach a heavy bolt to one end of the line and a light washer to the other end. Hold the spool so the light washer is on top. Holding on to the string with the heavy bolt dangling below, swing the light washer over your head in a circle. Now let go of the string attached to the bolt. The bolt will rise, pulled up only by the circular motion (centrifugal force) of the light washer.

☺ ☺ ☻ EXPERIMENT: What Do You Weigh On Jupiter?
On a more massive planet like Jupiter you would weigh more than you do on Earth, because Jupiter has more gravity. But on a smaller planet like Mercury you'd weigh less than you do on Earth. Use this cool online calculator to see what you weigh on the other planets: http://www.exploratorium.edu/ronh/weight/

☺ ☺ ☻ EXPERIMENT: Roller Coaster Challenge
Get at least four 6 foot sections of Styrofoam pipe insulation, a marble, and a roll of masking tape. The challenge is to create a working roller coaster with at least one loop and one turn. Along the way, discuss problems and discoveries. The kids will discover things like the need for the loop to be lower than where they dropped the marble from. And if they needed more speed, then the height of the initial track line had to be increased.

☺ ☻ **EXPERIMENT: Friction's Speed Limit**

You need a die cast car and a ramp. Send your car down on to a smooth wood or linoleum floor. Observe how far the car travels. Now send your car down the same ramp on to a carpet. Observe how far the car travels this time. Why does the car go further on the smooth floor? If you sent the car off in a zero friction environment what would it do?

☺ ☻ ☻ **EXPERIMENT: Hover Craft**

Make a hand held hover craft. Air has friction too, but it has much less than a solid surface. Make a balloon car to demonstrate this.

You need a balloon, an old CD, a spool, like from sewing thread, and some glue, like Gorilla Glue or super glue.

1. Glue the spool directly to the CD, lining it up with the hole.
2. Let the glue dry.
3. Now put the end of the balloon over the spool.
4. Blow up the balloon through the spool.
5. Let it go, CD down, on a smooth surface.
6. The CD will skate all over the surface until the balloon runs out of air.

For even more fun try to make a full size, human carrying version of the balloon car. On the next page you can see one our dad made for the grand kids. It uses a leaf blower to provide a cushion of air. (There are lots of versions of specific instructions for this online!)

Additional Layer

Some animals are designed with friction in mind.

Think about fish or birds or cats. Identify some streamlined animals.

On the Web

Visit:
www.sciencekids.co.nz/gamesactivities/friction.html

to experiment with how different surfaces affect the force of friction on a moving car.

Definitions

There are three types of friction:

Sliding: two objects that touch each other as they slide past.

Rolling: wheels cause a much smaller surface area of the weight of an object to contact a solid surface, making for less friction.

Fluid: the friction experienced against a liquid or a gas, like the friction of the air on an airplane.

Friction Game

Play a friction game all day. As you go about your life identify and point out occurrences of friction. Award a point for each identification.

Small candies dropped in a dish make for excellent point keepers and also provide the award at the end.

Additional Layer

Look at this interesting friction problem. Nathan is on the 4-wheeler, which is equipped with chains to give it greater traction on snow, while CJ is seated in a sled, which requires low friction.

☺ ☻ EXPLORATION: Household Friction

Look for places around your house where friction is an issue. Consider cars, bicycles, the bathtub (don't want to slip), the outside walk when it's wet or icy, the spinning drum in your dryer, and many more. In some places we want friction and in others we don't. How do we overcome the friction problems in each of the places you found around your home?

☺ ☻ EXPLORATION: Wheels

Wheels are a way to overcome friction. Think about how a wheel reduces the friction and makes it easier to move an object vs. dragging it across the ground. Try it out for yourself. Pick a heavy object and try to move it by first dragging it, then by putting it in a wagon or wheelbarrow to move it. Which is easier?

EXPLANATION: Friction in Space?

Whatever else there is out there in space, there is no friction. If there were, the planets would slow down and spiral into the sun. That would be bad. Talk about global warming!!

THE ARTS: MORAL STORIES

Storytelling is an ancient tradition. For ages stories have been used to transmit ideas, values, morals, and ethics. Storytelling and writing have become a great forum for much larger issues than the story itself. Themes of love, goodness overcoming evil, peace, family, religion, society, truth, and justice, among others, can be portrayed through simple plots. Stories can teach us and make us think. They can make us want to be like the hero or heroine. They can instill in us a desire to be better than we are.

Moral stories are intended to teach us a lesson. Some of the greatest teachers in the world taught their lessons through stories, because while straight preaching will be quickly dismissed, a lesson within an interesting story is more easily swallowed.

Moral stories come in several forms, most notably, parables and fables. A parable is a story that is specifically designed to teach a bigger religious or moral principle. It uses a real life, everyday occurrence that just about anyone can relate to. Biblical parables are the most famous, but non-religious works can be parables too. In a parable, each part of the story represents something else. Parables are full of symbolism.

A fable is a brief story that illustrates some moral principle. At first the two seem the same, but there are differences. Fables don't typically use familiar, everyday happenings. Instead, they tend to focus on the imaginary, using talking animals or animated objects as their characters. The lessons in them are not allegories. The characters don't represent something else; instead, the reader learns by the example of the characters. The parables of Jesus Christ and Aesop's fables are some of the furthest reaching stories ever told.

☺ ☻ ☻ **EXPLORATION: A Grand Metaphor**
Parables can be seen as metaphor on a grand scale. A metaphor compares two objects and often parables do the same. Read the parable of the sower from Matthew 13 and record what each element of the parable represents. You can use the printable from the end of this unit.

Sower:_____
Seeds that fell by the wayside:_____
Seeds that fell in stony place: _____
Scorching sun:_____
Seeds that fell among thorns:_____

Teaching kids the meanings of common phrases and sayings can be really fun. We generally have a saying of the week. I always write the saying up and have the kids read it, then guess what it might mean.

On one side of a paper the kids write the saying and on the other side draw a picture of what it means.

Learning common phrases is partly a matter of cultural literacy, but it also lends itself to developing thinking and reasoning skills. Our phrases often lend themselves perfectly to a great writing or art assignment. Often we look up the origin of the phrase and have a brief lesson in history or literature to go along with it. Whenever possible, I also connect them in some way to a unit we are studying.

This week we are finishing up a unit on oceans, and the saying "a fish out of water" was very easy to relate to that course of study.

Karen

Thorns:_____
Good ground:_____

What is the overall message of the parable of the sower?

This is a good parable to start with because the second half of the chapter (Matthew 13:18-23) provides the answers! If you want more of a challenge, read more of the New Testament's parables and try to decipher what they represent.

EXPLANATION: Symbol versus Allegory
In moral stories, symbolism and allegories both play a major role, but the two things are not the same.

A symbol is a word, place, object, or character that represents something else beyond the literal level of the story. A stop sign is a symbol. It is just a piece of metal shaped like an octagon that is painted red. Literally, it means nothing. Symbolically, it is quite significant though. Without it, our streets wouldn't be nearly as safe. Without some sort of concrete symbol, how could we communicate the more vague concept of "stopping" to drivers? It would be difficult indeed. A symbol can function all on its own.

Allegory is a network of symbols, all working together to reveal meaning deeper than the story itself. One symbol on its own cannot be an allegory. An allegory could just be read as a story, but its intention is to teach using double meaning. The word allegory actually derives from "allegoria" in Greek, which means, "speaking otherwise." The next exploration about the men and the lamb is a perfect example of an allegory. One who is wise will see the greater meaning in the story and apply it to himself, but it could also just be taken as a story.

☺ ☺ ☺ EXPLORATION: The Rich Man, The Poor Man, and the Lamb

Briefly tell the story of King David sending Bathsheba's husband to the front lines of the war so David could escape the consequences of stealing his wife, and then read 2 Samuel 12:1-7. This is the parable that was meant to help King David see the wrongs he had committed. Create stick or paper bag puppets of the characters and let the kids re-tell the story.

Discussion Questions:
- What did Nathan (the prophet telling King David the story) mean when he said, "Thou art the man"?
- Why was it easier for King David to see the lesson in the story than to see the same lesson he was overlooking in his own life?
- What do you think King David might have done if Nathan had just come out and told him how immoral he was being?
- Why do you think moral stories like parables are effective?
- You haven't done the same things King David had done, but does the story still apply to your life in some way?
- Could it somehow have meaning for every single person who reads the story?

☺ ☺ ☺ EXPLORATION: The Parable of the Banquet

The Parable of the Banquet is found in the Talmud: "A king invited his servants to a banquet without stating the exact time at which it would be given. Those who were wise remembered that all things are ever ready in the palace of a king, and they arrayed themselves and sat by the palace gate awaiting the call to enter, while those who were foolish continued their customary occupations, saying, 'A banquet requires great preparation.' When the king suddenly called his servants to the banquet, those who were wise appeared in clean raiment and well adorned, while those who were foolish came in soiled and ordinary garments. The king took pleasure in seeing those who were wise, but was full of anger at those who were foolish, saying that those who had come prepared for the banquet should sit down and eat and drink, but that those who had not properly arrayed themselves should stand and look on." (Shabbath 153a).

Discussion Questions:
- What do you think the moral of the parable is?
- Can you find more than one meaning?
- Who does the king represent?
- What does the banquet represent?

Additional Layer

During the Middle Ages allegory was a big part of the Christian culture of Europe. They waxed very eloquent upon defining and analyzing and beating to death the allegories of the Bible all while tying their philosophy to Classical scholarship.

There are four types of allegory:

Literal: Historical fact

Typological: connecting and comparing the Old Testament to the New Testament

Moral: How one should act

Anagogical: dealing with future events to come such as the resurrection

Famous Folks

Ivan Krelov was a famous fabulist of Russia. Look up some of his stories.

Explanation

Often when we start a new unit study I give the kids a homemade booklet that accompanies the unit. When they're done we have books to add to our classroom library that not only document what we've learned, but also give my kids the sense that they are not just students, but authentic writers as well.

I keep the books pretty simple. Yesterday we started a unit on important world landmarks. I created a very simple book for them and took it to our copy center where I paid one dollar to have it coil bound.

Inside are pictures of each of the landmarks we'll be studying, printed from various sites online. I also added a place for them to write the name of each landmark as we study it, answer questions interspersed throughout, and write a few interesting facts on the blank sheets. The last page is a world map to mark each of the locations of the landmarks.

Karen

• Can you think of another story that illustrates the same message?

Illustrate this parable and then re-tell it in your own words.

☺ ☺ ☻ **EXPLORATION: The Blind Men and the Elephant**
This parable comes from an old Buddhist tale, which explains an important part of Buddhist philosophy. See if you can spot the point of this tale (there is more than one point made here).

The story goes that six blind men came up to an elephant and discovered what it was like, relying only on what they felt in front of them. One man, feeling the side of the elephant, declared it to be like a brick wall. The second man felt its tusks and decided the elephant was like spears. The next man felt the elephant's tail and was certain the animal was like a rope. The fourth man touched the ear and declared an elephant to be like a fan. The next man felt only the trunk and was certain the elephant was like a snake. The final man reached out and touched the elephant's legs, certain that an elephant was just like tree trunks. For hours the blind men argued about what an elephant must look like. No one was willing to listen, completely convinced of what they had felt. Finally, they decided to visit the wise man of the village and learn what he had to say. He said, "Each of you is right and each of you is wrong. You see, you each touched only one part of the elephant, therefore you have only a partial view. Put each piece together and you will understand what an elephant looks like." It is often very difficult for us to see things from anyone else's point of view.

Picture by Itcho Hanabusa, a Japanese artist (1888)

Re-create what the elephant would have "looked like" to the blind men had they put their views together. Each component of the elephant is made with their observations. A wall for a body, a rope for a tail, a fan for an ear, spears for tusks, a snake for a trunk, and tree trunks for legs.

Talk about what the moral of the tale is and why it can be difficult to see someone else's point of view.

Try it yourself. Choose a large object (we recommend making a construction with chairs, blankets, a broom, and so on), blindfold the kids and have each one touch and describe a different part.

☺ ☺ ☺ **EXPLORATION: Aesop**
Aesop was a man who lived in ancient Greece. He was a slave and a storyteller. Some books say that he was able to win his freedom because he entertained his owner with his clever stories. Some people say that he didn't really exist at all because he didn't actually write down his stories. They believe that Aesop was just the name given to anyone who told fables. Still, there are quite a few ancient texts that describe him and reference his fables.

There are many versions of his famous fables, which teach moral

Picture from a woodcut, frontispiece of a Spanish edition of Aesop's fables (1489)

Additional Layer

American poet, John Godfrey Saxe, wrote a poem based on the parable of the Blind Men and the Elephant, creatively called *The Blind Men and The Elephant.*

Additional Layer

James Thurber wrote modern fables, morals and all, in *Fables For Our Time.* Check it out!

JAMES THURBER

Fables for Our Time
and Famous Poems
Illustrated

Fabulous Fact

Today people read fables to children to entertain them, but Aesop wrote them as political and social commentary.

Fabulous Fact
The word "fable" comes from the Latin "fabula," which means little story. Someone who tells or writes fables is known as a fabulist. The word "fabulous" originally meant "pertaining to fables" but now people mean amazing or outstanding when they say fabulous. Kinda makes you feel differently about the title of this sidebar, doesn't it?

Additional Layer
Baby swans are called cygnets. Swans mate for life. Swans live all over the world and migrate from mid and upper latitudes to warmer equatorial latitudes during the winter. What else can you find out about swans?

Photo by Jim Champion, CC

Fabulous Fact
According to our Greek historian friend, Herodotus, Aesop was tossed off a cliff by the people of Delphi who were displeased with Aesop for unknown reasons.

lessons. One of the reasons we have so many versions is that the stories were told over and over again, but not written down until much later and by many different people. Here are some you should definitely read:

- The Boy Who Cried Wolf
- The Tortoise and the Hare
- The Fox and the Grapes
- The Ant and the Grasshopper
- The Town Mouse and the Country Mouse
- The Lion and the Mouse
- The Dog and the Manger
- The Dog and His Shadow
- The Wolf in Sheep's Clothing
- The Goose and the Golden Eggs
- The Maid and the Milk Pail

After you read each fable, have the kids try to guess what Aesop's moral of the story was. Then do an activity to go along with the story. Here are some activities to try:
- Read three fables. Write the name of the fables on index cards and the morals on index cards. Try to match the stories to their morals.
- Put on a play of the fable.
- Do a puppet show. At the end, have the puppets hold up a sign telling the moral of the story.
- Read different versions of the same fable and compare their similarities and differences.
- Illustrate the fable.
- Write your own version of the fable.
- Write your own fable with a different story and different characters, but the same moral.
- Make stick puppets of the characters.
- Pretend to be one of the characters from the fable and write a letter to someone else about your experience.
- Make a paper plate or paper mache mask of one of the characters.

☺ ☺ ☻ EXPLORATION: Talking Animals
One of the characteristics of fables is that the characters are usually animals. Why do you think this is a good learning tool for teaching morals? Do people generally like to be told what to do? How does using animals soften the message? In literature, we call this device anthropomorphism, which is just a really big word

that means "human form" because the animal characters in the story are just like humans. Another word for this is personification. We take an animal and we make it seem like a person by giving it human traits.

Often the animals used in the stories represented human traits or characteristics. Draw several animals and label them with characteristics they might represent. Here are a few fill-in-the-blank comparisons to get you started:

Lion : Proud
Fox : Tricky
Fish :
Dog :
Whale :
Turtle :
: Wise
: Silly
: Humble
: Smart

☻ EXPLORATION: The Ugly Duckling

Hans Christian Anderson was the first to write down this fable of a swan who was raised by a duck. He was the ugliest, most awkward of his siblings and felt terrible about himself and unloved all through his youth. Then one day while gazing into the pond he sees a reflection of a beautiful swan. He realizes it is himself and is amazed at his own beauty and the acceptance he finds among the other swans.

Make a swan from a paper plate and paper. First fold the paper plate in half. Then cut hand prints out of white paper. Staple the hand prints to the back side of the paper plate to make a tail. Then cut a long oval from the white paper and fold it in half, attaching to the

other end to make the neck and head of the swan. Glue on a triangle beak in orange and wiggly eyes if you'd like.

You might also try an origami swan. It is one of the simplest of origami projects. Many tutorials can be found online.

Additional Layer

The Labyrinth of Versailles, a maze on the royal grounds of the French palace, was built on the orders of Louis XIV in 1665. A few years later Charles Perrault, the great author of fairy tales, advised the king to install 39 statues representing the fables of Aesop.

PLAN DV
LABIRINTHE
DE VERSAILLES.

Each of the statues was also a fountain, having jets of water coming from the mouths, representing speech. Also at each statue was a poetic quatrain explaining the piece. The whole thing was extremely intricate, colorful, magical, and expensive.

Too expensive for even Louis, who had the whole thing torn out in 1778.

Famous Folks

Portrait by Per Kraft the Elder (1767)

Ignacy Krasicki was a Polish bishop of the Roman Catholic faith. He was born into a noble family, received an excellent education, was very influential with kings and popes, and was instrumental in the Polish Enlightenment.

Additional Layer

A Mullah is a man educated in Islamic law and scholarship. Often such a person would be the spiritual leader of a community, such as a cleric or a mosque leader.

A mullah with some female students

☺ ☺ ☺ EXPLORATION: The Mouse and The Cat

Another teller of moral stories was the Polish writer Ignacy Krasicki. He wrote a volume called *Fables and Parables*. Here is one selection:

A mouse, which had eaten a whole book some time ago,
Felt that he had absorbed everything there was to know.
He addressed his companions: "I'll relieve your alarm;
Depend on me, and the cat will cease to do us harm!"
They sent for the cat; and the latter, ready ever,
Wasted nary a minute in coming to confer.
The mouse launched into his sermon. The cat was all ears
And sighed and wept... And the mouse, seeing the cat in tears,
Drew greater inspiration for his sermon from that;
And he emerged from his hole—and was caught by the cat.

What do you think the moral of this story is? Apply it to yourself.

☺ ☺ ☺ EXPLORATION: Nasreddin

In much of the world, stretching from China to the Swahili Coast of Africa and from the Balkans to the Middle East, Nasreddin is as common a figure as Aesop is to us. He, like Aesop, lived in a small village in ancient times. His homeland is generally thought to have been someplace in the Middle East, but the true facts have been lost to time. He told simple moral tales, usually humorous, but always with deeper meanings.

Here is one story told by Nassreddin:

A neighbor came to the gate of Mullah Nasreddin's yard. The Mullah went to meet him outside.

"Would you mind, Mullah," the neighbor asked, "lending me your donkey today? I have some goods to transport to the next town."

The Mullah didn't feel inclined to lend out the animal to that particular man, however. So, not to seem rude, he answered:

"I'm sorry, but I've already lent him to somebody else."

All of a sudden the donkey could be heard braying loudly behind the wall of the yard.

"But Mullah," the neighbor exclaimed. "I can hear it behind that wall!"

"Who do you believe," the Mullah replied indignantly. "The donkey or your Mullah?"

Look for the meaning behind the story (hint: the stories deal with human thought patterns more than human behavior patterns), then read more Nasreddin tales. Look for books by Idries Shah, especially *Tales of the Dervishes*, recommended in the Library List at the beginning of the unit. The story above has been widely retold, but can be found in *The Sufis* by Shah.

☺ ☺ ☺ EXPLORATION: More Moral Stories
For a large variety of moral stories, go visit www.moralstories.org. You can even write your own moral story and submit it to their website.

☺ ☺ ☺ EXPLORATION: Storytelling Festival
To celebrate your unit on moral stories, hold a storytelling festival. Each participant should prepare at least one moral tale to tell orally.

Make a program, announce the storytellers, and serve treats. You may even want to invite a few extra spectators to come hear the tales and cheer on the storytellers.

Writer's Workshop

Choose 2 of the famous storytellers from this unit and write a compare and contrast essay on the way they tell moral stories.

Is one or the other more effective at telling the story?

Is one or the other more effective at teaching the moral?

Do you think the way the story is received is dependent on culture?

Additional Layer

Many stories have morals – folk tales, fairy tales, classics, and even many of the novels you pick up off the library shelf. Any time you read a story you should ask yourself what the message is and decide whether or not it is a good, moral message. It's the moral messages that we should fill our minds with, while avoiding the garbage books.

Coming up next . . .

Unit I-8

Assyrians - Deserts
Fluids - Rhythm

My Ideas For This Unit:

Title: _____   **Topic:** _____

_____

_____

_____

_____

_____

_____

_____

_____

_____

Title: _____   **Topic:** _____

_____

_____

_____

_____

_____

_____

_____

_____

_____

Title: _____   **Topic:** _____

_____

_____

_____

_____

_____

_____

_____

_____

My Ideas For This Unit:

Title: _____   Topic: _____

_____

_____

_____

_____

_____

_____

_____

Title: _____   Topic: _____

_____

_____

_____

_____

_____

_____

_____

_____

_____

Title: _____   Topic: _____

_____

_____

_____

_____

_____

_____

_____

_____

A Phoenician Ship

The Phoenicians were expert sailors and traders. They settled along the Mediterranean Sea and made money by trading with areas all over the Mediterranean and beyond. They were known for their beautiful purple cloth and for their cedar wood.

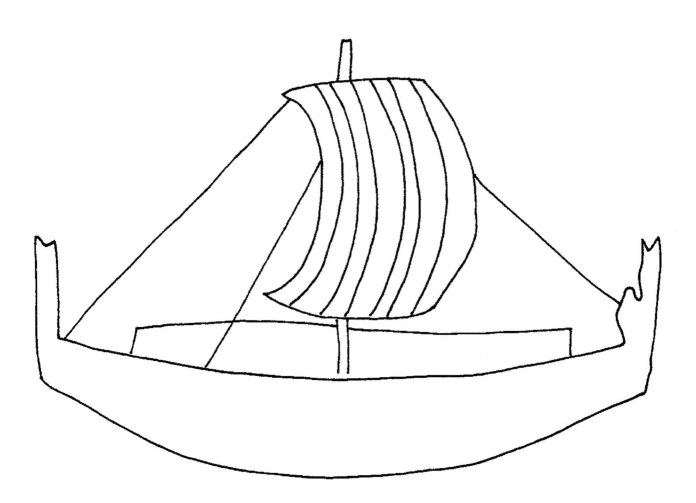

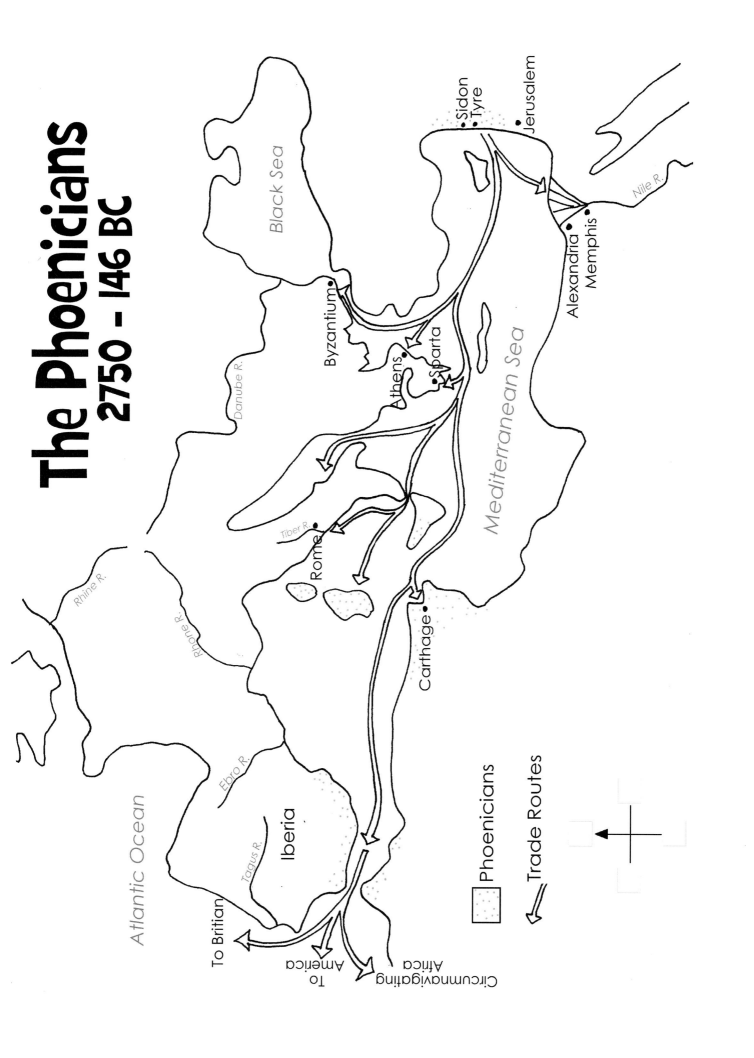

The Phoenicians
2750 - 146 BC

Atlantic Ocean

Rhine R.

Rhone R.

Ebro R.

Tagus R.

Iberia

To Britian

To America

Circumnavigating Africa

Carthage

Rome

Tiber R.

Danube R.

Black Sea

Byzantium

Athens

Sparta

Mediterranean Sea

Sidon

Tyre

Jerusalem

Alexandria

Memphis

Nile R.

Phoenicians

Trade Routes

Phoenicians: Unit 1-7

2750 BC 1-7

Founding of Tyre

1500 BC 1-7

Settlement of Cyprus

1300 BC 1-7

Trade treaties with Egypt

1200 BC 1-7

Tyre becomes foremost of Phoenician cities (concurrent with the Trojan War)

1100 BC 1-7

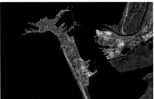

Cadiz and other colonies on the Atlantic coast are established

980 BC 1-7

King Hiram makes trade treaties with David and Solomon and sends out trade expeditions

876 BC 1-7

Phoenicians pay tribute to Assyria

813 BC 1-7

Founding of Carthage

636 BC 1-7

Eastern Phoenicians throw off Assyrian rule

538 BC 1-7

Becomes a province of Persia

500 BC 1-7

Hanno circumnavigates Africa

332 BC 1-7

Tyre falls to Alexander the Great, marking the end of the eastern Phoenicians

264 BC 1-7

Carthage begins Punic Wars with Rome

218 BC 1-7

Hannibal crosses the Alps with his army and runs rampant all over Italy

201 BC 1-7

Carthage falls to Rome

146 BC 1-7

End of the Punic Wars and end of western Phoenicians

Phoenician Alphabet
Compared to Latin Alphabet

Highlight every place you see similarities. Then, write someone a note using the Phoenician symbols and give them this key to solve the note. If there are letters you need that are missing, add them to this sheet. The Phoenicians did not have all 26 letters that we do.

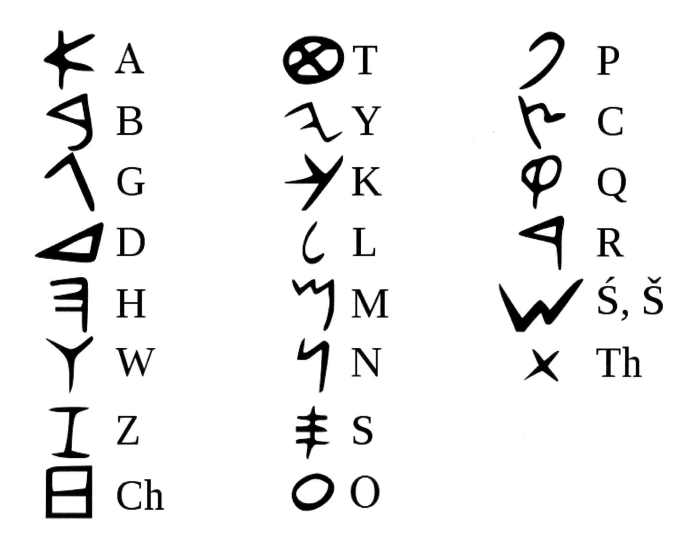

The World

Sea Trade Routes

Coastal Formations

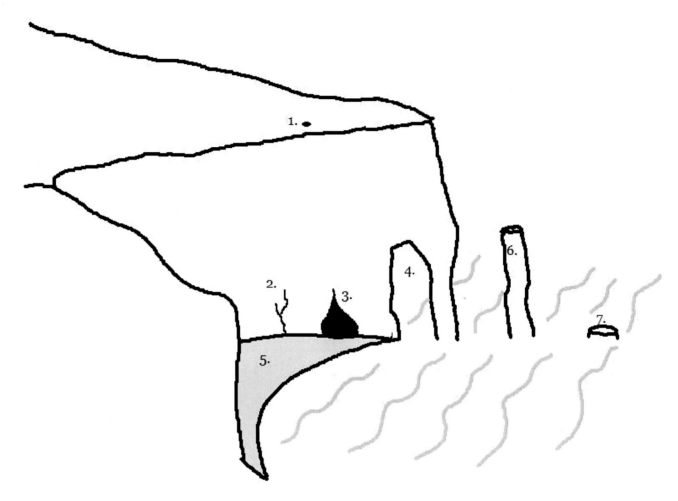

Label the numbered formations on the picture above. Below is a word bank and a paragraph describing the formations to help you:

Blow Hole	Sea Cave	Sea Arch	Sea Stack
Beach	Stump	Fault or Joint	

These formations are made through erosion. The sea waves hit the coast over and over and over until the rock wears away, weak spots are formed, and caves and arches are carved out. Eventually an arch may collapse, leaving a stack and then the stack itself collapses leaving only a stump. Beaches are formed from bits of rock or coral worn down and broken up into small grains or pebbles. A blow hole is an opening reaching from a cave below to the cliff top above the sea. Blow holes are formed when a weak spot, a fault, is opened up more through the action of the waves bursting into the cave.

Sea and Coast Crossword

ACROSS

1. Much larger than a bay; open sea surrounded by land.

3. Smaller than a bay, a piece of land between two bodies of water.

5. A high prominent piece of land that rises over the sea on a rocky coastline. Lighthouses are often placed here.

6. A narrow piece of land between two bodies of water and connecting larger pieces of land.

9. The largest bodies of salt water on the planet.

11. A small area of sea surrounded partially by land.

DOWN

2. A long, narrow inlet of the seas between tall rocky cliffs.

4. A piece of land that juts out into the sea, being surrounded on three sides by water.

7. A deep, sheltered bay which can be used as a port for ships.

8. Sometimes used interchangably with ocean, a large body of water smaller than an ocean.

10. A pointed piece of land that projects from a coastline.

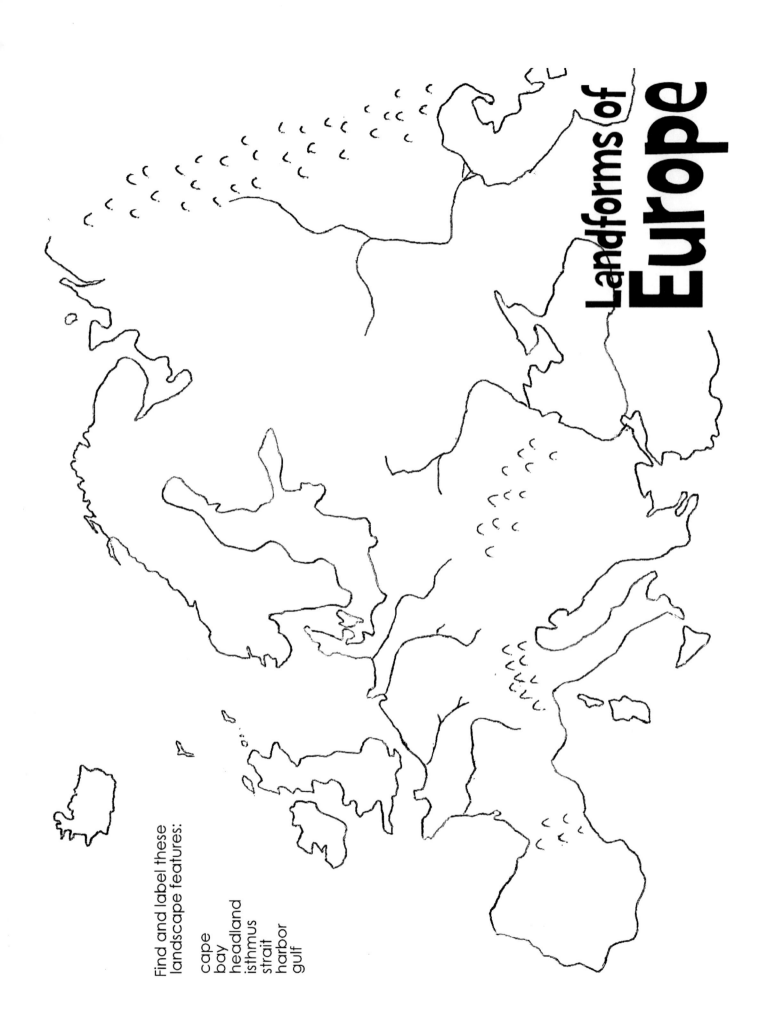

Landforms of Europe

Find and label these
landscape features:

cape
bay
headland
isthmus
strait
harbor
gulf

Galileo and Gravity

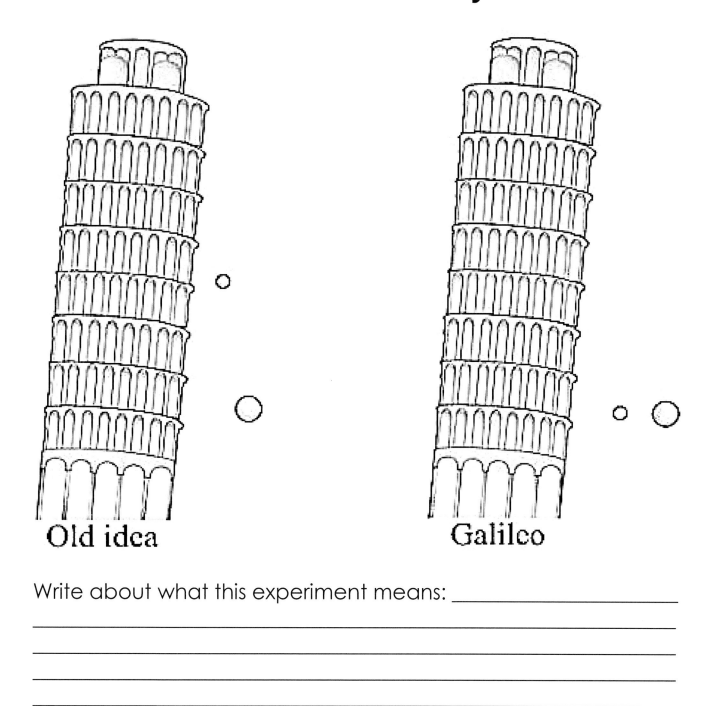

Old idea   Galileo

Write about what this experiment means: _____

_____

_____

_____

_____

_____

_____

Illustration courtesy of Theresa Knott.

THE SOWER

Read Matthew 13, then write what each of these items in the parable represents:

Sower:_____

Seeds that fell by the wayside:_____

Seeds that fell in stony place: _____

Scorching sun:_____

Seeds that fell among thorns:_____

Thorns:_____

Good ground:_____

What is the overall message of the parable of the sower?

_____
_____
_____
_____
_____
_____
_____
_____
_____
_____
_____

ABOUT THE AUTHORS

Karen & Michelle . . .
Mothers, sisters, teachers, women who are passionate
about educating kids.
We are dedicated to lifelong learning.

Karen, a mother of four, who has homeschooled her kids for more than eight years with her husband, Bob, has a bachelor's degree in child development with an emphasis in education. She lives in Utah where she gardens, teaches piano, and plays an excruciating number of board games with her kids. Karen is our resident Arts expert and English guru {most necessary as Michelle regularly and carelessly mangles the English language and occasionally steps over the bounds of polite society}.

Michelle and her husband, Cameron, homeschooling now for over a decade, teach their six boys on their ten acres in beautiful Idaho country. Michelle earned a bachelor's in biology, making her the resident Science expert, though she is mocked by her friends for being the *Botanist with the Black Thumb of Death*. She also is the go-to for History and Government. She believes in staying up late, hot chocolate, and a no whining policy. We both pitch in on Geography, in case you were wondering, and are on a continual quest for knowledge.

Visit our constantly updated blog for tons of free ideas,
free printables, and more cool stuff for sale:
www.Layers-of-Learning.com

Made in the USA
San Bernardino, CA
31 October 2018